ELECTRONIC EVIL

POISON ON THE COMPUTER SCREEN

ROXTA CHARAN

ISBN 978-1-68509-265-8

For all the software engineers (including the author of this book), who were once a victim of cybercrime.

Also, for those cybercriminals over there.

Contents

FOREWORD

Can we secure the world from a Bloodless War?

I'm talking about CYBER-SECURITY.

As the world is inreasingly Interconnected, everyone shares the responsibility of securing Cyberspace!

PREFACE

The stories in this book are truly fictional and no event mentioned in any of the stories are not true as far as my knowledge.

Even though, the author of this book is a software engineer, he doesn't like computers at all. He thought that he might be watching by someone else. That is exactly, what is called Cybercrime.

This book contains two stories that are completely related to Cybercrime.

I

Not Found!

A man nicknamed Eiken came to India from a small country termed, Micronesia in a plane. He came for an influential work that was assigned to him. Micronesia is a small country, but it has an airfield in a state named, Pohnpei. Eiken is from the same state. The security guardians in the airport examined Eiken before allowing him to enter India. They noticed nothing vulnerable with him. They reviewed the passport also, and that is a legitimate passport. They allowed that Pohnpeian man to enter India. He went to the place where he was assigned and began doing his work.

A month later, Eiken completed his task and planned to travel to his native home. Unfortunately, cops were hunting him and he tried a lot to escape from them. Cops were following him because he killed a celebrity at his home. From the moment he landed in India, he began preparing to shoot the celebrity. The task assigned to him was to destroy that celebrity. Eiken was a contract shooter and his job is to shoot the souls by taking some coins. He disappeared from the cops and went to the airfield to go to his natal place. At the airport, he requested the Ticket Issuer to provide him a ticket to Pohnpei. The ticket issuer checked and said, "There is no such destination point with the name, Pohnpei". Eiken got shocked and asked the issuer to check it once more. The issuer re-checked and surprisingly said, "There is no such place in the map also. How come you came from there?"

Eiken was confused as he heard that the place he came from was missing. He started pondering about what would have happened to his state. Many things were rolling in his mind which caused mental depression to himself. He thought any tsunami occurred in Pohnpei and that devastated the state. He was worried about his family as he was thinking the tsunami would have destroyed their place. There was no news in India about the tsunami in Pohnpei. So, he convinced himself that the tsunami would not be the reason for Missing Pohnpei. Eiken was suffering from the thoughts he was getting about the missing state.

A few days later, Eiken got a call from an anonymous number. He answered the call and understood that the language spoken by the other person is Pohnpeian. By that, he realized that the people of the state were still alive. But, he could not understand what the other person on the phone was speaking. So, Eiken said, "I sohte wehweke, Menlau pwurehng nda", which means, "I don't understand, please say it again" in Pohnpeian language. The other person on the phone asked, "Is this Eiken I am speaking with?" Eiken replied, "Yes, It's me Eiken. Can I know who are you? The other person answered, "I am your mother"

Eiken felt relaxed and asked, "How are you Mummy, Is everyone fine over there?

His mother responded, "Yes Eiken, everyone and everything is super fine here. When will you come here?"

Eiken answered, "I will come super soon to see you, Mom. How's our state, Pohnpei?"

His mother clarified, "Pohnpei is also super cool and developing a lot these days."

Eiken asked, "is there any new state formation soon?"

Mother answered, "No such thing, son. Pohnpei is not going to be divided at all. Is there any problem, son?"

Eiken doesn't want to make his mom tensed and so, declared, "Nothing, Mom. Will come soon to meet you, Bye." and stopped the call.

After the call, Eiken felt relaxed because his family was breathing. Now, his only thing is to get back to his place as soon as possible. He is in a circumstance where he could not go to the cops and complain about the disappeared Pohnpei as he did the crime. The cops were hunting for Eiken to arrest him. So, he changed his style along with the face to complain to the cops about the lost Pohnpei. Wherever he goes to complain, everyone laughed at him as the complaint was silly and the seriousness of the issue was known only to the one who was enduring it, that is Eiken. The cops thwarted Eiken about the complaint he was trying to give. Eiken with grief, shouted, "Menlau!", which means, "Please". He went to many police headquarters in the city he was in, but no one understood his complaint.

In the last police station he went to, he noticed a lean man with curly hair using two computers at a time. On one computer, he is seeing the world maps and on the other computer, he is writing code. Eiken got a doubt and went to that lean man and asked him, "Is it possible to erase a state from the map using codes?" The lean man answered, "Yes, it is achievable. If we can draw lines on the map, then we can remove some lines on the map too." Eiken asked, "Can anyone do that. Is it that simple?" The lean man replied, "No, it needs so much knowledge on hacking. Why, is there any problem?" Eiken told him that Pohnpei was missing and asked him whether he can get that back. The lean man replied, "Yes, it can be done by the one who erased. I can just help you by discovering the one who erased." Eiken appreciated him for the help he was doing.

The lean man commenced working confidentially to find the person who deleted Pohnpei. The hacker was using many powerful firewalls, so it is challenging to get hacked by someone. So, the lean man was failing to find the unethical hacker. On the other hand, Eiken originated listing his foes who would have made him stopped in India. As he was a contract killer, he got so many villains on the list and he could not discover the one who is a hacker. He knew that the goal of the hack was to erase the Pohnpei and to make him struck in India. By that, he filtered out the list of the enemies in India. Now, he got only one person whom he killed a few months before. Now, he inquired as cops about the software engineers in the celebrity's surroundings. They gave him the specifications of 4 software engineers. Now, Eiken started investigating the 4 software engineers one by one in a room in an apartment.

First, he asked the first Software engineer, "What is your name?" The first engineer replied, "I am Alex." Eiken asked, "Do you do coding well?" Alex replied, "Yes, I do. Anything needed?" Eiken asked, "I want a hacker who can hack Google." Alex replied, "I cannot do hacking. I am from the support team who just copy-paste codes to solve any issue." Eiken told him to get out and to send the other one.

The second software engineer came in the room. Eiken asked him his name. He replied, "Mera Naam Sohail hai." Eiken asked, "How well do you do coding?" Sohail replied, "Jab koi requirement clearly diye tho main code likhta. Koi requirement hai tere pass?" Eiken told him that he wants a hacker who can hack Google. Sohail said, "Main hack nahi kar sakta hoon." Eiken told him to get out and send the next one.

Eiken asked the third engineer her name. She said, "This is Alima." Eiken asked her, "What is your job in IT?" Alima replied, "My job is to do testing after the code was developed." Eiken asked her whether she can hack something. She said that she could not hack. Eiken told her to send the last one. She went out and sent the last one inside.

Eiken asked the last engineer his name. He said, "My name is Aswad and I am a hacker." Eiken asked him, "Can you hack Google and erase a state from the world map." Aswad replied, "Yes, I can and I did that once." Eiken asked, "Why did you do that?" Aswad replied, "To stop a man in India and to kill him because he killed my mother's brother." Eiken warned him, "Do you know who he is? He is a contract killer. He can kill you if he knew you did that." Aswad asked, "How do you know all that?" Eiken removed the mask and replied, "Because that was me. Now, you should put the erased state in the same location, or else you would be erased from this world." Eiken sent the other 3 to their respective houses and went to Aswad's house along with him. There, Eiken tied up the family of Aswad tightly with a rope and blackmailed Aswad to place Pohnpei in the exact location where it was previously.

Aswad placed the state, Pohnpei in the exact location by hacking Google and maps again. Eiken released his family and went to the airport wearing a new mask. Aswad booked a plane ticket to Eiken with his own money and sent Eiken to his home.

Finally, after a very long struggle, Pohnpei was retrieved to the world map. From then, Eiken stopped killing people without any reason.

II
A.T.D

On 2020-07-19, a man reviewed his bank balance on his computer. It was 50K Euro. Within few seconds, his bank balance increased to 3.5 Lakhs and the man was so happy about that. At the same time, on the other hand, a Father in Aragon, Spain went to his house so grievously. His family members asked him what had happened, but the man did not respond to any one of them and wordlessly went to his bedroom and locked the door. His girl was feeling terrified about him. She went to the window and saw inside his bedroom. There she noticed a rope hanging to the ceiling fan to which her dad was hung. Due to that, his entire family went into deep grief and confusion about why had he killed himself. The girl called the cops and acquainted them with his father's death.

The cops came to the house and inquired the family about the father's death. They asked, "Do anyone of you know why he had killed himself?" The family said, "We don't know." The cops questioned them, "Do you notice any unusual these days?" The girl said, "Yes, we noticed one thing suspicious at the time he killed himself." The cops asked her, "What was the thing you found questionable?" She said, "My dad's discomfort. I've never seen my dad that much sadness in my whole life." The cop asked, "Do you know what caused him so sad?" She said, "No, I don't know." The policeman asked, "Did you try to request him what happened?" She said, "We begged, but he did not answer to any one of us." The cops examined the pockets of the father's shirt and trousers. They found some pieces of paper.

The cops, along with the family, worked a lot to bring all the pieces of paper together. Eventually, after more than 30 minutes of the efforts, they brought all the pieces together. They recognized that was an ATM slip. On the receipt, it was stated that Three Lakh Euros were withdrawn by the father. The cops questioned the family, "Do you know why he had withdrawn that much amount?" The spouse of the dead man said, "I guess, he had withdrawn for our girl's wedding." The cops imagined, "Burglary club would have stolen his money. Due to that, he was so depressed and killed himself." They went to the ATM from which the father had withdrawn the cash.

The girl requested the cops whether she can come along with them or not. The cops denied her request and went to the ATM. They noticed the CC camera at the ATM and asked the guard, "Is this CC camera working?" The guard said, "Yes, it's working super fine." The cops questioned him, "Where can we get the CCTV footage?" The guard gave them the details. The cops went to the location where they can get the CCTV tapes. Unfortunately, the office was shut as it was already 11 at night. So they went to the same office the next day morn.

The next day morning, cops went to the office and requested the administrator to give them the CCTV footage of the prior day from 7 PM. The administrator showed them the footage. The cops observed the footage so carefully and noticed nothing unusual there. The father went inside the ATM and swiped his card, took the slip, and came out. By that, they believed that in the midway, his cash was stolen by the robbers. Since it was the profit of his several years' hard work, and he could not control his pain and so, killed himself. They closed the case as self-destruction.

The girl requested the cops to discover the robber who caused the grief to her father. She continued, "By that, at least the law would last." The cops understood her and began hunting for the thief. They started searching in the CCTV footage of the CCTV in the route from the ATM to his house. Luckily, his complete traveling was recorded in several CC cameras. The cops watched the recordings, but unfortunately, the cops noticed no one other than the father on that path. They went back to their police station. Surprisingly, many people were waiting to give a complaint. The frontman in the queue wrote the complaint as "I went to the ATM to withdraw a small price of 5K. I got the slip, but I did not get the cash from the ATM." Everyone in the queue said, "The complaint is the same, but the amount lost is different and from different ATMs."

The cops were surprised by their complaints and asked, "Did the amount subtracted from your bank account?" They said, "Yes sir. That's what the problem is. Please solve the mystery as soon as possible." The cops did not believe their reports and complaints and went to an ATM. One of the cops swiped his debit card to verify what was happening. He entered the smallest amount to withdraw cash from the ATM and entered the PIN. Within few flashes, a receipt came in which it was stated that the amount was withdrawn. The cop verified his bank balance, unfortunately, the amount got subtracted. The cops were shocked by that and confused. The cops were trying to solve the mystery, but they failed.

Regrettably, similar complaints were recorded in every region of Spain. No cop was able to unlock the puzzle. The cops in Spain understood the seriousness and petitioned the government to close the ATM temporarily till the ATM puzzle was solved. So that, people may not lose their money. Since the initial victim was the hung father, the cops thought that the mystery would have happened few moments before the father tried to withdraw the money. Therefore, the cops went to the office where the CCTV tapes were stored and requested the manager to show the recordings of 2020-07-19. The cops started watching the footage from that day till the father came there.

Within few days, the story became Continental, which means similar cases were registered in the places of the entire Continent. The cops were unable to know who the hell is doing that. The cops in Aragon, Spain were watching the tapes to find some trace. Many people went to ATMs on that day, no one was found suspicious except a man. The man with a hoodie but no mask on his face went behind the ATM and did something illegal there. The cops suspected that guy and began hunting for him. After few days, cops caught the man with a hoodie who was the suspect for the ATM story. The cops showed him the recording and asked, "What were you doing behind the ATM?" The hoodie man replied, "I won't disclose what I did that day." The cops forced him, "Will you say now without any torture or will you say after the torture?" The hoodie man did not reveal the secret.

The cops took the hoodie man into a separate chamber and started 3rd-degree treatment on him. The cops lacerated him by cutting his nail with a cutting-plier, beating on his limbs with the clubs for 2 days. The guy was almost finished and opened his lips to reveal what he did that day. He said, "I inserted a chip in the ATM." The cops questioned him, "What was that chip? What does that do?" The hoodie man said, "I don't know what that does, but I got some gold for doing that." The cops asked him, "Who demanded you to insert that chip there?" The hoodie man said, "A French guy. He texted me in Kik messaging app."

The policemen asked, "What did he message you?" He replied, "He would send me a code. I need to copy that into a chip and need to insert that in the most adjacent ATM. I would get some huge quantity of gold for doing that." The cops asked, "Do you know what that code includes?" He said, "No, I don't know. I am not a sofware engineer." The cops offered the hoodie guy, "If you transfer the code right now and remove the chip from the ATM, we'll leave you." The hoodie man got tempted by the proposal. He sent the code to them and removed the chip as per the agreement. The policemen cheated the hoodie man and did not leave him. Similarly, the cops caught all the people in that region who inserted the chips in the ATM and get them removed.

By knowing that, every cop of the other region and other country tried to find the man who inserted the chip. They also get it removed. From that time, all the ATMs were re-opened. But the man who made people insert the chip and what does that chip do was still a conundrum. The cops took that code and went to the Cybercrime Department to understand what that code does. The officer asked the cops for 5 days to understand the code. The cops gave him the time he demanded. After 5 days, the cops went to the officer for the information about the code.

The officer said, "This code will debit the money from one bank and Deposit the same money in another bank account automatically." He added, "He made the ATMs as ATD. I mean, Any Time Deposited." The cops asked the officer, "To which account, the money will be credited?" The officer gave the account number and the account name to the cops. The hacker's name was Kevin, the world's top hacker. The cops, along with the cybercrime ethical hackers attempted a lot to hack Kelvin's bank account. But they failed many times as they were using outdated equipment. Hence, the cops recruited the top 10 unethical hackers of the country and requested them to hack the bank account of the hacker who changed the source code of the ATMs. All together tried a lot for more than 5 days, but could not hack him as he was using the most secure firewalls and the most frequently changing pin for his bank account. Finally, on the 7th day, the hackers hacked the hacker and stolen his money with the support of the government.

The hackers decided to share the money among themselves without informing the cops. As they decided, they shared all the stolen money among themselves and escaped from the region. The policemen were not the children to leave them, they traced the phone numbers of all the 10 unethical hackers and located where they were at that time. By the unluckiness of the hackers, all the 10 unethical hackers were staying at the same place and they didn't use any location-changing software. By that, the cops caught them easily and took all the money they've stolen from Kelvin.

The cops took all the money and shared it across the governments of all the countries. The Spain cops threw all the 10 unethical hackers behind the bars with some lesser punishment as they helped in hacking Kelvin and getting back the stolen money. Spain government informed the French government about Kelvin and requested them to arrest him in the high-security prison without any technical types of equipment.

ABOUT THE AUTHOR

The author of this book is Charan, well known by his pen name, RoXta. He writes many different stories. Some of them are related to real life crimes and some of them are truly fictional.

This book is a fictional book which can become true in the coming future.

RoXta is not a professional author, but a passionate artist. He is very passionate in learning different arts like Drawing, Rapping, Writing stories, Photo/Video editing, Photography and many more.

RoXta is a software engineer who has a phobia called Robophobia (fear of Robots/Computers). He is fighting with his fear everyday to overcome his fear.

In order to get relief from the work stress, he used to learn different arts.

FINALLY...

Cybercriminals are the other kind of theifs who stole the information in different ways. Everyone knows that the information is wealth. If it was stolen, entire life of one can be stolen by them.

Beware of cyber threat just by not sharing any valuable information to anyone.

I would like to thank each and everyone who read the book till here with a lot of paitence.

www.ingramcontent.com/pod-product-compliance
Lightning Source LLC
Chambersburg PA
CBHW060523090326
40690CB00068BA/4358